Little

Wet-

Paint

Girl

MINGLING VOICES
Series editor: Manijeh Mannani

> *Give us wholeness, for we are broken. But who are we
> asking, and why do we ask?* —Phyllis Webb

Mingling Voices invites the work of writers who challenge bound-
aries, both literary and cultural. The series issues a reminder that
literature is not obligated to behave in particular ways; rather, it can
defy convention and comfort and demand that readers summon the
courage to explore. At the same time, literary words are not ordinary
words, and the series implicitly raises the question of how literature
can be delineated and delimited. While Mingling Voices welcomes
original work — poems, short stories, and, on occasion, novels —
written in English, it also acknowledges the craft of translators, who
build bridges across the borders of language. Similarly, the series is
interested in cultural crossings, whether through immigration or
travel or through the interweaving of literary traditions themselves.

SERIES TITLES   *Poems for a Small Park* • E.D. Blodgett |
Dreamwork • Jonathan Locke Hart | *Windfall Apples: Tanka
and Kyoka* • Richard Stevenson | *Zeus and the Giant Iced Tea* •
Leopold McGinnis | *Praha* • E.D. Blodgett | *The Metabolism of
Desire: The Poetry of Guido Cavalcanti* • Translated by David R.
Slavitt | *Kiyâm* • Naomi McIlwraith | *Sefer* • Ewa Lipska, trans-
lated by Barbara Bogoczek and Tony Howard | *Spark of Light: Short
Stories by Women Writers of Odisha* • Edited by Valerie Henitiuk
and Supriya Kar | *Kaj Smo, Ko Smo / What We Are When We Are* •
Cvetka Lipuš, translation by Tom Priestly | *From Turtle Island to
Gaza* • David Groulx | *Shape Your Eyes by Shutting Them* • Mark
A. McCutcheon | *Grieving for Pigeons* • Zubair Ahmad, translated
by Anne Murphy | *Little Wet-Paint Girl* • Ouanessa Younsi, trans-
lated by Rebecca L. Thompson

Ouanessa Younsi

Little Wet-Paint Girl

Translated by Rebecca L. Thompson

◊ AU PRESS

Copyright © 2018 Mémoire d'encrier inc.
English translation copyright © 2022 Rebecca Thompson
Published by AU Press, Athabasca University
1 University Drive, Athabasca, AB T9S 3A3

https://doi.org/10.15215/aupress/9781778290060.01

Originally published in French as *Métissée* (Mémoire d'encrier, 2018).

Cover and interior design by Natalie Olsen, kisscutdesign.com
Printed and bound in Canada

Library and Archives Canada Cataloguing in Publication
Title: Little wet-paint girl / Ouanessa Younsi ; translated by Rebecca L.
Thompson.
Other titles: Métissée. English
Names: Younsi, Ouanessa, author. | Thompson, Rebecca L., translator.
Series: Mingling voices.
Description: Series statement: Mingling voices | Translation of: Métissée.
Identifiers: Canadiana (print) 20220286914 | Canadiana (ebook)
20220286930 | ISBN 9781778290060 (softcover) | ISBN 9781771993722
(PDF) | ISBN 9781771993739 (EPUB)
Subjects: LCGFT: Poetry.
Classification: LCC PS8647.O955 M4713 2022 | DDC C841/.6—dc23

We acknowledge the financial support of the Government of Canada
through the Canada Book Fund (CBF) for our publishing activities and
the assistance provided by the Government of Alberta through the Alberta
Media Fund.

For Louise G.

The girl screamed that she had neither heart nor face
and that she had been betrayed from the beginning.

ANNE HÉBERT

You live as two equal parts.
You are neither you,
nor anyone but you.

MAHMOUD DARWISH

Come on, Ouanessa.

Let's save the dead child.

There are nights inside us.
You have to watch out for them.

NICOLE BROSSARD

When I was born, spirits flew from my head,
their fingers stained in noise. They whispered
Souk Ahras Souk Ahras without protecting me
from the lion. In Montréal, the snow deepened
like milk poured over the city, and I was restless.

I refused the breast. I wanted morphine, trauma.
Receding ghosts, venomous little saints

whispering *Souk Ahras Souk Ahras*

like sand over the city.

Voices reached me from behind the curtain of sleep. Those whom I would become, far away, would not let me be.

I fought with faulty weapons. Heads rolled like clementines, tumbled into the Medjerda.

Awakening.

I arranged the nightmare on a coat hanger. Emptied the closets of memory one by one.

Sunburned side of the world: I drank my father's dreams.

I walked on my hands. My feet had been
chopped off in the middle of the night. By whom,
no one knew, and there was no investigation.
I was an orange girl with a weird name.

I hadn't been woken up by the red smell, but I
felt my tendons in my dreams.

In the morning, I was stunned to find my feet
gone. I searched everywhere: under blankets
of cold, in my brother's stomach, in front of
masked faces. Nothing. They were lost.

My father forbade me to look for them.

The children of the Rue de Chasseurs sold
lemonade. I sold my lungs and my name.

Little Wet-Paint Girl. Wherever the century
touched my skin, it erased a little of my colour.

And I let it, like a false mother.

On my birthday, scorpions wormed their way
through the gifts. I unwrapped dolls and stings.

The venom shot arrows into my liver.
A mysterious fever poured into me.

To survive, I kidnapped hope's children.
That was a mistake.

To this day, one of those mothers hunts me,
escapes from me.

In kindergarten, they nicknamed me *chocolat*
because I was the brownest girl in the class.
A fennec fox ran down my legs.

My father had kinky hair. Curious people would
pay to touch it.

Did he dress himself in that cloak of shame?

As for me, I don't dress up anymore. I'm nostalgic
for a lie.

At seven, I read my father's first name on a form.
I discovered that I'd been spelling it wrong,
confusing *z* and *d*. My father wasn't my father.
A letter separated us.

Where was he hiding? Who was this stranger
who had taken his place?

I put up a missing-person poster in the red-light
district. No one contacted me.

I always search for my father in women's tombs.

Among tall grass and wasps, I didn't know the wind was an hourglass. My innocence amused the woman next door. Her delight planted watermelons, pink mouthfuls amidst famine. We rescued different species, different riddles:

Why does September make you thirsty?

Once born, who stays behind?

The neighbour woman was a theatre.

We grew older, and I lost her by losing myself.

In primary school, a kid told me I was dirty.

For months, I washed away my doubts under
a shower of bleach. Dermis, tissues, muscles,
bones. I rubbed, scraped them all, until my soul
was scoured as white as a tooth.

A tooth in the mouth of my sorrow.

To be no more than snow. And to somehow
still be?

My parents peeled me like a fig. I was a different
fruit each day.

I would continue the motion, peeling away my
colour, my tongue, my roots. At age twenty,
I disappeared from my own story, and later,
the story confirmed my absence. We celebrated,
laughing, a cake of stings and molars.

I became a blank page. I paced the city, sliced it
up like bread. I was escorted by falcons, and I
spoke to them in an inaudible dialect.

Coming across a foreign shape, a pockmark on
the surroundings, I recognized my own skin.

And I continued down my path, peeling my fear
like an apology.

In the courtyard I was digging a secret tunnel to
Souk Ahras. Tulips, bulbs, worms: windows that
I crawled through without shattering reality.
Sometimes my heart slipped up into my throat
with the effort. I chewed on it like an eraser.
A new one would germinate, made of ladybugs
and poppies, and I continued my work. I drank
gulps of clouds and was poisoned.

My flesh fell away, a too-big skirt. The strikes of
the shovel wore me out. I persisted. I wanted to
see the iris of the globe and my uncle inside it.

My parents were preoccupied with my health.
They nursed me with leeches, sermons. I dug
deeper, deeper as if my fate depended on it —
and my fate depended on it.

Holes in the earth, holes in the page: I needed a
life of my own, just one.

An orange tree grew through walls of windows.

I wanted to uproot it, return it to the other side of the world – Souk Ahras. Impossible. It was metallic, a mirror.

It grew and grew, demolishing the church, the school, the train. The countryside transformed into a huge fruit tree.

I tried to raze it, summoned the titans of denial, assembled saws for a delicate demolition. It was all in vain. An orange tree bloomed in the room of the past.

Resigned, I sat under the tree to rest. It vanished.

I became botanical, more myself than ever before.

I tobogganed all the way to Souk Ahras. Outside,
the storm wrapped the earth like a present.

Hot peppers repelled monsters. I had killed the
violence — ha-ha! — that lay naked in my bedroom.
At bath time, I rinsed myself with turmeric and
felt every breath run down my flanks.

At twilight, the things we miss stroll through
libraries like cats. I emptied trash cans and
memories onto the ground. No one picked
them up.

I waited patiently at the beginning of the story,
alone before the words.

Near the tree-branched swimming pool of my family tree were syringes.

Sometimes I buried them. At other times, I'd trade my limbs for these perches. My wooden leg seemed more myself than the rest of me.

Roots, bark, sap, the branches weighed me, steady as concrete below.

At twilight the flora came alive, gaining flesh and free will. A forest of my ancestors stared while I brushed away my blight and my rust.

I watched them too, hoping through a trance

that my unknown family would kidnap me.

To run away with the family that didn't exist.
The one that existed was nowhere to be found.

Like that one, I evaporated little by little. Only
my skin resisted. I creamed it with toothpaste,
the difference between painting and transparency.

Something unseen made me chew snakes. I hid
under draped sheets of bronchi, I begged for a
hand and a stump was offered.

My only wrist, floating in Souk Ahras.

My song served as dinner vocal cords and angel hair. For dessert, my eyes, carob cookies.

After the meal, I left my sun-browned skin on a coat hook. My nose pressed up against the memory like a squashed mouse.

And my mouth? What is a mouth, anyway?

My disappearance began again.

How to run away: escape not with the cat, but within the cat. In a purr. Shinny up the ladder of a meow.

Gnaw at parasites, hunt epidemics and rats. Leave hairs all over October, moulting: turtle-scale, claws, freedom.

And before dozing off curled like a fetus, gaze with cat's eyes

at the poem burning like a little girl.

The executioner cut me in two. I woke up with fig branches for arms.

I examined the stumps for a while. I didn't lie down, neither on the table nor on the clay earth. A sightless eye watched me, and I felt it leaving scars on my cheeks.

I know nothing of crime or my stolen share. I want the share that isn't held responsible.

In a toy box, I search for her headless body.

Mother without elbows, father without knees,
and I couldn't colour in my own name. I was
borderless on the map of a face.

Outside the lie seduced the truth. They both
flung clumps of cartilage at human walls.
Bruises, graffiti.

I needed to scream, scream, but I had neither
voice nor I.

I tried to learn my father's language. The sounds leapt from my lips, atomic jackrabbits. I tried to pronounce my first name. *You're saying it wrong.* I persevered. I had to puncture the cornea of these words.

The language remained a memory. My father shouted it down my throat. I was afraid of it, and afraid of the white plates that shattered against the kitchen floor.

My voice was cut out. I forgot how to use it.

I kept speaking like a bonfire.

I scribbled poems in my mother's room. I couldn't write anywhere else, inside my secrets or my father's exile.

That room isn't a place anymore. Nostalgia destroyed the furniture, and the blue horse lies buried.

I got older. My hand no longer existed.

I still write within my mother's body.

Each morning, I received mail from Souk Ahras.
A family made of ink saved me from denial.

The envelope seemed thin and the address
nonsense: Rue des Chasseurs, where fairies
stumbled.

At night, as soon as my parents passed away,
two parts of me made love without touching,
like dragonflies. Trembling, I sealed the empty
envelope that I mailed to myself.

Then I fell asleep, heart intact, at the very least.

At age eleven, I opened a letter from Caroline,
who was born in Souk Ahras to an Arab mother
and Québécois father. I had sent the letter.
I acted out her part.

Caroline didn't speak French, and no one
understood where her name was from.

Her hands were nothing but wrists. Her parents
had cut them off at birth so she could never write.
She would write anyhow.

She was a psychiatrist over there. There, that
meant nothing. There, no one ever turned out to
be sick.

I thought about Caroline, I played with Caroline,
I became Caroline, both impossible and necessary
like unicorns, God, and fairy tales.

Like prayers whispered to no one
are to the mother.

In a house of grey and turquoise, there were
no mirrors. No one could see their own face,
no one had a face, and seeing was not the same
as feeling.

Outside, infinite reflections laughed. Store-
mirrors, shrub-mirrors, neighbour-mirrors
watched me. I became a girl.

I melted under it all, half human and half sorbet.
The mirror ripped the ligaments from my soul,
butchering me like moose meat.

Trapped in that house, I lived in fear that my
real name would be revealed.

In the whole city, only one house had walls.
They called it the cemetery. My family lived there.

The walls. They had seen Algeria. You could
also find them among ruins, among wars. And in
Germany, where my parents would get married.

Kisses by the thousands, like bullets, shredded
into the women who wanted those bricks torn
down.

Today my parents are divorced, and my childhood
home isn't a home anymore, just walls.

I'm not there anymore, either.

Camellias of consonants, imaginary date-palms…
did I write this garden?

I touched fables of crystal. I swam to the surface
of the heart. Someone somewhere built a vault.
I didn't help.

Someone else stole me in the night. Not a thing,
me. I discovered the thief. It was me.

A tale buried in the nerves of the father.

He is buried, too.

My nails grow into my father's body. I traced my first words in his shadow, inserted mistakes into our names.

On his temples I drew my first sketches: our legless ancestors, snowy lions. Illusions more solid than the void.

A family of seashells.

Inside the little girl everything crumbled:
her collarbones ripped through her lungs.
Her organs burst, grew back, and were
destroyed again.

She had to cling to her face so it wouldn't spill,
spreading like wine over the world.

We have to love the things that fall.

The trip had to happen. I packed my bags: cages, skin grafts, and the coffin that followed me like a mother.

Did my family recognize me? Were they still living, or had they succumbed to the enigma?

I didn't go.

My childhood lives inside this unbreakable vase that I'll never glue back together.

II

the self bathes in absence

MOHAMED YOUNSI

I drink memories.

SYLVIA PLATH

Was this self of mine a foreigner, or was it them?

I cut out the question. On the beach, blurry: spleen, intestine, pancreas lying among the crayfish.

Over Souk Ahras and Montréal the same fossils rained down.

I exhumed exiled bones.

My father's tears.

When I was tiny, I became responsible for the insulation and clotheslines. From Montréal to Souk Ahras: stretch the pelts. Certain people spoke sickness to me. Some were mercenary. I said nothing back, munching cherries of silence. I treasured pink hatchets and wooden bumblebees, and I hated the rumours humming across my skin.

The wind didn't shake me. I shook the wind.

Every Friday another cyclone took off, hanging the clothing of corpses over the ocean.

When I was microscopic, my mother's name and cord disappeared.

My brother and I were sailors, and our couches were rafts. Smurfs, cupcake dolls, and trolls sailed with us toward the mirage.

The tide swept the floor away. A giant piranha watched us. We had to stop the armchair from capsizing against a rocky atoll. We couldn't risk our ankles in the foamy sea.

Our parents meandered through the continent. Where was Souk Ahras hiding?

I was five, and I didn't know that girls of my age littered the Mediterranean like chunks of plasma.

My brother and I were not sailors. The couches were not rafts.

Childhood was true and truth was false.

The basement loomed, dark as in the beginning.
Suitcases, mops, teddy bears: objects spread
their jaws wide. Sometimes the river seeped in,
and pikefish caught hold of my gums.

In the centre of all this sat a statue of a fisherman
and his line. My uncle? From the walls, living
portraits of dead ancestors watched me.

In this room I tasted peppercorns of mercury,
I devoured words and lymph.

I met Ouanessa in this room.

In the cellar of solitude, I composed Souk Ahras
for sand and fog. Gazelles, camels, cheetahs...
I inherited a desert.

In this mysterious town all the men became my
father, all the women my mother, and I was the
mixed girl. I shed my skin in seismic tremors.

My grandmother Ouanessa watered victims and
grapevines. At the market they traded olives
and buttermilk. Then the night came, tattooing
Souk Ahras in henna.

And Ouanessa opened me, shattering herself like
stained glass.

I was a character in someone else's dream.
To stay grounded in time, I sculpted birds and
climbed dunes of origami.

The other slept. I didn't sleep anymore.
My body's scaffolding escaped me: my biceps
came undone, my vulva crumbled, my windpipe
grew into a cedar. Only my underground skin
and my rainbow femurs lasted.

I was a character in a dead girl's dream.

As soon as it snowed, I gathered only July.
I burned like harissa on the tongue. If I spoke up,
wild animals struck me down.

In every storm, Ouanessa came to see me.
She offered a sunbeam of quartz and spice;
she was my grandmother. And when I collapsed,
Ouanessa fixed me with prayers and pistachios.

For my grandmother had become the unnamed
meaning behind the name we shared.

Every month, Grandma Ouanessa's skull grew in my uterus, then trickled out in cranberry drops. My faith didn't look like a berry at all.

I cut off my breasts to starve the tumours. I threw them in the river. A willow tree ate my shoulder, and I lived on within the ancestors of paper.

A century later, Ouanessa learned to sew with her mouth.

The moon sketched a hot crescent from Souk
Ahras to Montréal. The sky didn't close that
night's-eye.

I looked for the grave of my grandmother, killed
by her heart at thirty-two, ripped apart by a son.

The muscle continues to beat in protest.

And Ouanessa patches me back together with
skins of rage and a thread of a poem.

Rosebushes grow over Ouanessa. There were clubbed owls, construction zones of crossed-out words. I grew older surrounded by appearances.

Ghosts hung from the stars. I cried, a little girl wrapped in their wings.

I watched the abyss.

The abyss held my gaze.

Ouanessa slept in amniotic fluid. She had neither past, nor future. I wanted to bring her back to life, but I was in chains, mauled by jackals.

Help! Help me!

Beauty didn't react. She just combed her reflection.

Today if Ouanessa sleeps, murdered, it's because of silence.

Pain disfigured my vagina. Purple milk, curdling,
overflowing like a volcano, scorched.

A monstrous dwarf clawed at my walls. Black
bass swam upstream in my stomach, undeterred
by doctors — pale beasts — who prescribed
medications as they grazed in their pastures.

Was this the dead woman trembling within my
name? Or was this the fetus lost in my uterus like
a whiplash lost in patience?

I didn't know. The truth seeped through, and so
did I, as liquid as vanilla.

Armed with a mirror I explored raspberry cliffs
and crags

and watched myself drip, covered in primroses,
from the lips of an ovary.

On the brink of bleeding, I raved madly,
convinced of my own infertility. Souk Ahras
would end here.

I threw my brain against a window. It rolled,
rolled, collected filth, storks, bottles.

It came back to me full of the tales I'd drunk —
playing pirates, bogeyman, Bluebeard; chewing
arsenic marshmallows.

Giving birth to the childhood was my consolation.

Jellyfish dried up on my chest. Fear gave way to a singular desire.

I floated between Souk Ahras and Montréal. A ghost ship rotted in the depths of tragedy. From a porthole, a saltwater grandma waved.

My fingers lashed like eels. I tried to capture them, but I got tangled in seaweed.

Back at home, I washed palms full of sharks and regrets, not my hands.

Crosses dotted the countryside. A new church
overlooked the ocean, summoning the faithful
and the faithless. Prayers popped like balloons.

In the crowd I picked out foggy ancestors.
What was that woman screaming, the one with
my name? What was that father murmuring,
haunted by tunnels?

A lion gutted my sight. Mystery left my tongue.
My teeth shattered.

There, the war went on. Here, peace endured. Maybe a parent died under a bomb, maybe a soldier smothered a child under a mauve pillow.

No one knew where my uncle lay.

There are ashes at the border. A corpse spills verbs across the page.

At ten I learned that my grandfather had died.
I also learned his name: Mohammed. I was more
shaken by his name than his death. I didn't know
him, either in Algeria or in myself. Every day,
I dreamed up a new grandpa.

Mohammed had one missing hand and one
normal hand. As he aged, the former grew back
and the latter wore away. No longer distinguishing
between the whole hand and the partial one, he
cut them both off with a sabre. His granddaughter,
who was passing by at the time, took the blood
for juice and drank it.

Since then, green slashes of loss

grow like cacti.

The rumour: my uncle Mourad was a colonel during the massacre. The racism: he passed down dangerous DNA. The reality: I swallowed raw tarantulas of amnesia.

Mourad was a name without a face.

Love him like a loss.

Glimmers of light shone through the fires I'd lit in my hair.

I clung to an illusion — was it my aunt Elseghira or my mother's bloody breast? — giving electroshocks. Now memory snaps the neck of the story.

Snowflakes fall in my memory, my body ripped apart by Elseghira.

I roamed through a maze of names. Spirits pierced my flesh, leaving legends and pebbles for me.

I devoured their truth, the teeth of God, like dice.

Little girl, I drew their bones and gnawed them down.

Ghosts snapped the house's tibias. My father set forgetfulness-traps. Spirits skirted around them and took human forms.

My nerves crumbled like chalk.

I watched the lie go off like a firework.

The film of my birth.

Our genealogy unrolled from my father's skull like a garland. Baptisms and bodies littered town squares, parks, hopscotch grids.

They were renounced, and it crushed them. When my inattention pressed down on them too, their shadows stained, stained, stained me.

As if I was dirty, as if I am dirty, as if nothing washes me clean.

I've been afraid ever since then of destroying ghosts. My own. Those of others.

The ones I create.

The dead lined up, plates at the ready. From their
cemeteries from Souk Ahras to Montréal, they
longed for cumin, they begged for wheaten doves.

The feast was at my house, the feast was me.

We cooked, cooked more, couscous and tagine
and merguez sausages of dust. At the centre of
the buffet were harissa and my father's remains.

I hoped to see my grandmother, born in Sakiet
Sidi Youssef and deceased in Souk Ahras, but her
recipe no longer existed on this earth.

The dead lined up and I wandered among them,
a little cannibal with no grandma and no stomach.

The end of the world. I watched for the apocalypse,
my palms deboned like cutlets. Lightning bolts
poured into my glass and I drank them without
an esophagus.

Sometimes a hazy Algerian uncle called out to me.
I didn't reply.

A camel made of ashes broke through my reality.
I fell silent, watched the inferno, watched meteors
and titans of hatred. I fell asleep, sure I was dead,
surprised by the breath that whistled through
my dreams like bullets.

The next day, the world still existed, but I didn't.

I was putting out fires in the living room. I put one out, but then another caught in a photo album. I couldn't find a fire extinguisher. I hid the cat in the piano.

Maman had taken maman away. Papa had taken papa away. And the basement held my brother hostage.

I apologized to the past.

I fought fires in the living room.

I was exhausted but I kept growing, ripening
with my phantom limbs.

They shared bites of matlouh, savoured hazelnuts,
apricots, cactus pears. These fruits embodied my
father, and they ate them. He bled, holey as a lake.

I fought off sleep, afraid that the ghosts would
snag the knit of my dreams.

To save myself, I drowned myself in the pond
of an O.

The headlines crushed my phalanges. I poured
sugar into a cup full of teeth, Souk Ahras in
light coffee.

I stirred the city with a spoon. I sipped its
outskirts. My father poured me a fresh thought.
I didn't confess to him what it was.

Swords appeared across my throat, though I was
not a forest.

I contemplated the corpses in an empty
room. The door wouldn't close — aunts, uncles,
grandmothers, grandfathers, all lay in a heap.

An unknown family called to me thought the
flutes of our veins. Incomprehensible streams
ran through me.

The empty rooms emptied out again. My aunties?
Maybe dead, maybe alive, I had no idea, and I
didn't recognize the colour of my skin, and that's
why I tore it off

like I rip away the fiction of my memories.

Why dismember the carcass of absence?

I dug up imaginary roots. I examined the horizon
not to see it, but to feel my eyes.

Armed with autumn, I waited for cliff-eagles.

Absence taken form.

The muscles behind the motion, I scraped
away epitaphs until I drew blood. Under the
inscriptions syllables emerged — Elseghira,
Mourad, Mohammed whispered to me of loss.

Young ancestors encircled me. I was full of
centres. The light leaked sound, but I wasn't
worried.

I was drawing closer to my roots, and my future.

How could I remember these women I'd never met? I grew up in their shadows, brushing against the translucence of their tunics.

Chili peppers tasted of famine and sand. Camels refused to wear their blinders.

My father lost his mother tongue, and I lost my father's tongue.

Loss was a language.

The years held me by the scruff. Dawn's face was burning. Death's face was frozen. Writing drove me back and forth from one to the other.

Fickle animal, would I ever go to that city of mint? Would I go, in my madness, with these women who were unknown but adored?

The clamour of my life.

And so I spent my childhood opening coffins.
There were still intact incisors and eyelashes,
there were centipedes of mystery.

I dishonoured nothing. I didn't eat the dead.

I only wanted to burn in the gravity of it all.

Maybe no poem could replace what was unseen.
Trapdoors formed from imprints in my memory.

No one saw its birth. The desert was real, pita on
the ground.

Nothing remained but the sharp-toothed saws
behind simple gestures, terror

and goodness.

Come on, Ouanessa.

Let's save the living child.

Translator's Note

The translation of poetry is a long walk.

You seek some sort of origin, try to discover some text that fixes your feet firmly in one direction.

You look ahead at the landscape, try to get a look at the text's face, evaluate your expectations and aspirations, and then you make start making decisions.

Then you take a step. Then another.

If all goes well, if the origin was steady and the steps line up as required, you will end up at a destination. That's the process, defined as concretely and as specifically as I'm able: discover, decide, then step and repeat.

I discovered Ouanessa Younsi one August morning in 2019 because of an article by Dominic Tardif in the Québécois newspaper *Le Devoir*.

The article, dated November 2018, focused on prominent young women in Québécois poetry. Ouanessa Younsi's work caught my eye immediately — she spoke of phantom limbs, and of identity as being shaped by absence as well as presence. I was in a meditative place in my own life: I had just moved back to my hometown in western New York, was newly jobless and motherless, and was attempting to live authentically in a repressive and dishonest America. I read a few excerpts from *Métissée* and felt seen: I felt deeply affected at that time by people I missed, and by the jarring sensation of encountering things in my city that no longer felt familiar. I wondered what I had gained in my years away — and what I had lost — and how those changes were affecting me. I bought *Métissée* that afternoon. I immediately responded to the poems with wonder and curiosity. Younsi was telling me about places and things I knew, like snow and schoolyards, and things I didn't, like Arabic pronunciation and the twists of orange trees. I felt like I was holding her hand and walking with her and learning about her life in a way that had me looking more closely at my own.

Published in September of 2018, the prose poems in *Métissée* (Little Wet-Paint Girl) examine Younsi's identity as a French-Canadian woman born to a Québécois mother and an Algerian father, beginning with her birth, and moving forward chronologically. By analyzing her family and herself through the eyes of a child, Younsi attempts to locate herself within her culturally mixed family. This includes the little girl's craving for connection with relatives she has never met, and with "the sun-burned side of the world" these people came from.

Younsi has explained that the title of this book, the feminine term for a mixed-race person, refers to the mixing of ethnicities but also to the mixing of absence and presence. My goal in this translation is to communicate this overall message: the things that we feel are lacking in ourselves and our lives are just as crucial, and as formative, as those we know to be present.

Speaking as a woman of colour — a Muslim woman of colour — in Québec, Younsi provides a fresh voice in Canadian and Québécois poetry. She addresses rootedness, family, dispossession, and race in a visceral and contemporary ways through the fractured body and the hankering for a diasporic family she connects to most strongly through her namesake grandmother.

In *Little Wet-Paint Girl*, elements of the uncanny, combine with the grotesque to create an unsettling, yet riveting, world. Throughout the collection, Younsi resists the idea of the authority of concrete details or linear narrative, instead inviting the reader to search for their own points of connection. The text demands slow, careful reading, breath between each fragment. The effect is an experience of the text and its themes through a feeling of disorientation or uncertainty.

My translation also accents Younsi's psychological and anatomical imagery. By discussing herself as disparate parts, with pages discussing her teeth, her feet, her lungs, her voice, her legs, and so on, Younsi communicates the struggle of a narrator who is either decomposing or constructing her own self – perhaps both – before our eyes.

I began to translate *Métissée* after reading three poems, making three conscious decisions as I set out:

First, that I would translate the whole collection. I liked it, I liked its face and the way it tugged at my fingers, and I wanted to see where it led.

Second, that I would read it as I translated. The experience of reading a poem for the first time is irreplaceable, and that uncovering process, my own shifting relationship to the presence and absence Younsi describes, was something I wanted to try to capture. Aside from some polishing, this volume is meant to reflect that fresh, first encounter. Younsi writes through a child's eyes as she encounters trees and ghosts and lemonade stands and Souk Ahras; I wanted to mimic that (self-)discovery.

Third, I would translate on paper, with a pen in my hand. As a young translator still toying with routine, I felt that I couldn't examine intention, or the dichotomy between presence and absence, without the physicality of handwriting.

I have tried to maintain the meditative flow of Younsi's prose poetry. The work does not separate poems into discrete units but allows each reader to interpret the pacing and rhythm of the collection independently. In this way, Younsi begins the work of creation and directs the reader to reach a personal conclusion to that work.

In his essay "La Traduction de la poésie," Yves Bonnefoy cautions the translator against overvaluing the "fixed form" of the poem — that is, the written word, be it the word of the source text or the translation.[1] We should, instead, find what motivates the poem, relive the act that spoke the poem into being, and dissociate that from the words. The words are traces. The intention, the obsession, the desire, is that which occupies the space between impulse and utterance. When done sincerely, it becomes possible to occupy that space and to create a translation that is just as true, both in honesty and in clarity, as the source.

1   Yves Bonnefoy, "Translating Poetry," trans. John Alexander and Clive Wilmer, *PN Review* 46 (November–December 1985). Originally published as "La traduction de la poésie," in Bonnefoy, *Entretiens sur la poésie* (Lausanne: Diffusion Payot, 1981).

A good poem seems to hold a shred of the poet under glass, preserving their voice in the space between inspiration and language.

Readers may notice that at the beginning of this note, I spoke of *a* destination, not *the* destination, when working with a translation project. Texts don't have singular destinations in mind – that's too metaphorical, even for me – and it's hard to know when a translation is finished. I will say, however, to trust the poem.

If you find a space somewhere between the yearning that set the poem in motion and the utterance that preserves that yearning, if you echo that intention, and use the words of a new language to preserve it, you've begun to translate.

If you take that step, and then do it again, you will end up finding a bit of yourself fixed under glass, and you'll become part of the poem. Both present and absent within the poem, if you will. That was my destination.